W9-AHJ-466

WITHDRAWN

Whose Bones Are These?

Crime-Solving Science Projects

ROBERT GARDNER

Enslow Elementary

an imprint of

 Enslow Publishers, Inc.
40 Industrial Road
Box 398
Berkeley Heights, NJ 07922
USA

http://www.enslow.com

Enslow Elementary, an imprint of Enslow Publishers, Inc.

Enslow Elementary® is a registered trademark of Enslow Publishers, Inc.

Library of Congress Cataloging-in-Publication Data

Gardner, Robert, 1929–
 Whose bones are these? : crime-solving science projects / by Robert Gardner.
   p. cm. — (Who dunnit? Forensic science experiments)
 Includes bibliographical references and index.
 Summary: "Presents several forensic science experiments using trace evidence.
 Includes science project ideas and crimes to solve"—Provided by publisher.
 ISBN 978-0-7660-3248-4
 1. Forensic anthropology—Experiments—Juvenile literature. 2. Science projects—
Juvenile literature. I. Title.
 GN69.8.G37 2011
 614'.17—dc22
                                2008050089

Printed in the United States of America

092010 Lake Book Manufacturing, Inc., Melrose Park, IL

10 9 8 7 6 5 4 3 2

To Our Readers: We have done our best to make sure all Internet Addresses in this book were active and appropriate when we went to press. However, the author and the publisher have no control over and assume no liability for the material available on those Internet sites or on other Web sites they may link to. Any comments or suggestions can be sent by e-mail to comments@ enslow.com or to the address on the back cover.

Illustration credits: © 2009 by Stephen Rountree (www.rountreegraphics.com)

Photo credits: Associated Press, p. 8; courtesy of Cobus Steyl, p. 41; Joseph Moore Museum, p. 32; Life Art image copyright 1998 Lippincott Williams & Wilkins, pp. 27, 29, 33; © Mikael Karlsson/Arresting Images, p. 7; Shutterstock, p. 35.

Cover photo: Shutterstock

Contents

Who Dunnit?
Forensic Science
Experiements

Experiments with a 🎖 symbol feature Ideas for Science Fair Projects.

Introduction

Crime scene . . . forensic evidence . . . fingerprints . . . DNA. You probably hear these words often. Forensic science television programs show scientists solving crimes. Perhaps you would like to try it, too. But what *is* forensic science?

Forensic science is used to solve crimes. Its findings can be used in court. Scientists have to be very careful when they collect evidence. Evidence can put a person in jail. But some people have been found innocent and released from prison as a result of forensic evidence. In this book, you will learn about and practice some of the skills used by forensic detectives.

Entering a Science Fair

Some experiments in this book are marked with a 🎗 symbol. They are followed by ideas for science fair projects.

Judges at science fairs like experiments that are creative. So do not simply copy an experiment from this book. Expand on one of the suggested ideas. Or think up a project of your own.

The Scientific Method

Scientists try to understand how things work. They make careful observations. They do experiments to answer questions. Nearly all scientists use the scientific method. They: (1) observe a problem; (2) form a question; (3) make a hypothesis (a best-guess answer to the question); (4) design and do an experiment to see if the hypothesis is true; (5) analyze the results of the experiment; (6) if possible, form conclusions; (7) accept or reject the hypothesis. After their experiments, scientists share their findings. They write articles telling other scientists about their experiments and results.

How do you begin a project you can use in a science fair? You start by noticing something that makes you curious. So you ask a question. Your question might arise from an earlier experiment, something you saw, something you read, or for another reason.

Once you have a question, you can make a hypothesis— a possible answer to the question. Then you can design an experiment. The experiment will test your hypothesis. For example, suppose your question is "Do fingerprints fade away in sunlight?" You would place one set of prints in the sun, and one set in the dark. Both sets should be kept at the same temperature, be made on the same surface, and so forth. Sunlight will be the only difference between the two groups.

During the experiment, you would collect data by observing the prints. Does either group of prints start to fade? Does either group begin to change in any other way? You might take photographs of the prints every day. You would compare the data collected from the two groups over a few days. You might then be able to make a conclusion.

Your experiment might lead to other questions. These questions will need new experiments. That's the nature of science!

Safety First

To do experiments safely, always follow these rules:

1 Always do experiments under **adult** supervision.

2 Read all instructions carefully. If you have questions, check with the adult.

3 Be serious while experimenting. Fooling around can be dangerous to you and to others.

4 Keep your work area clean and organized. When you have finished, clean up and put materials away.

Blood Evidence

Blood: We all have it. Sometimes it becomes an important piece of evidence. Blood or bloodstains are often found at a crime scene or on the clothes of a suspect. There may be drops of blood, or spattered blood on a floor or wall. Bloody fingerprints may be found on doors or other places. What do scientists do with blood evidence?

A forensic scientist will examine spattered-blood patterns. The patterns may allow him to re-create the crime. From the shape of dried drops of blood, an expert can often tell the speed and angle at which the drops landed. He may also be able to decide the force of a blow or bullet that hit the victim. Cleaned up bloodstains may be made visible again by spraying with luminol.

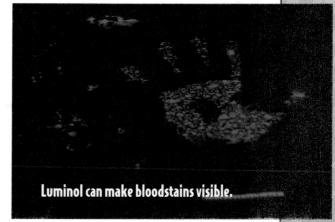

Luminol can make bloodstains visible.

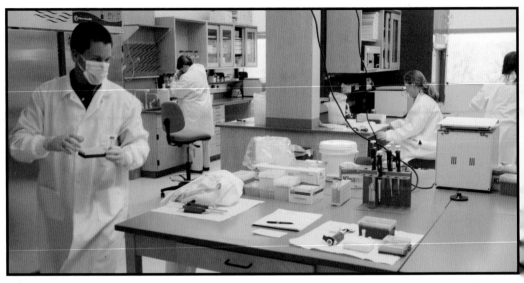

Evidence from a crime is analyzed in a crime lab. Usually, many scientists work to solve several cases at one time.

Luminol reacts with red blood cells. It makes a bluish glow that can be seen in the dark.

Blood found at a crime scene will be tested at a crime laboratory like the one seen in the photograph above. If it is human blood, the blood type (A, B, AB, or O) will be determined. It may match that of a victim or a suspect. If it matches a suspect, DNA testing may be done next.

As you can see, just a few drops of blood can provide forensic scientists with lots of evidence. Let's begin to learn more about it.

1-1 Blood Drops and Spatters

THINGS YOU WILL NEED:
- small glass
- warm water
- red food coloring
- teaspoon
- sugar
- eyedropper
- white paper
- ruler or yardstick
- tape
- waxed paper
- board
- books or bricks
- protractor (optional)

To see what can be learned from drops of blood, you can do an experiment.

1 Fill a small glass halfway with warm water.

2 To give the liquid the color of blood, add a few drops of red food coloring.

3 To give it the thickness of blood, add a heaping teaspoon of sugar. Stir the mixture.

4 Fill an eyedropper with the "blood" you have prepared.

5 Let a drop of "blood" from the eyedropper fall about an inch onto a sheet of white paper (see Figure 1a). What does the drop look like after it lands? As you can see, the drop flattens and spreads out when it lands. We say it spatters. Its new shape is called a spatter pattern.

6 Let blood drops fall on the paper from greater heights. Try heights of one foot, two feet, four feet, and six feet. How does height affect the drop's spatter pattern?

7 Make a "runway." Tape six or seven sheets of paper together end to end.

8 Let moving drops fall onto the "runway." Move the eyedropper sideways over the runway as you release drops of "blood" (Figure 1b). How does the horizontal (sideways) speed of the drop affect a drop's spatter pattern?

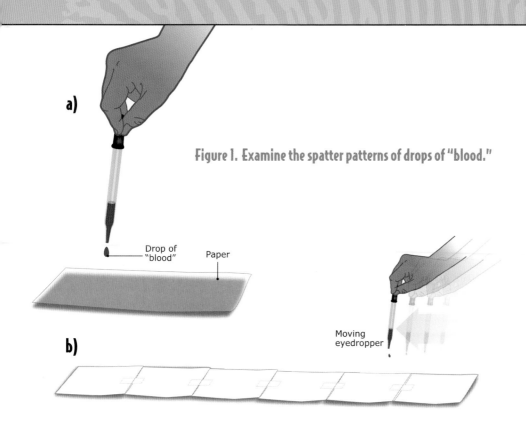

a)

Figure 1. Examine the spatter patterns of drops of "blood."

Drop of "blood"   Paper

Moving eyedropper

b)

How does a combination of different heights and different horizontal speeds affect the spatter patterns of drops of "blood"?

The spatter pattern of a drop moving sideways is determined by a law of motion. The law says that moving things will continue moving unless they run into something else. When the bottom of the drop hits the paper, the rest of the drop continues moving forward, making small streaks or "tails" (See Figure 2).

9 Let the drops fall onto waxed paper. Are the spatter patterns different on waxed paper? If so, why do you think they are different?

10 How will the angle at which a blood drop lands affect its spatter pattern? To find out, let drops fall onto paper taped to an inclined board (Figure 3a). When drops fall on the incline, they will hit the paper at an angle. How does the size of the angle (Figure 3b) affect the spatter pattern? If you have a protractor, you can measure angles from 0 to 90 degrees.

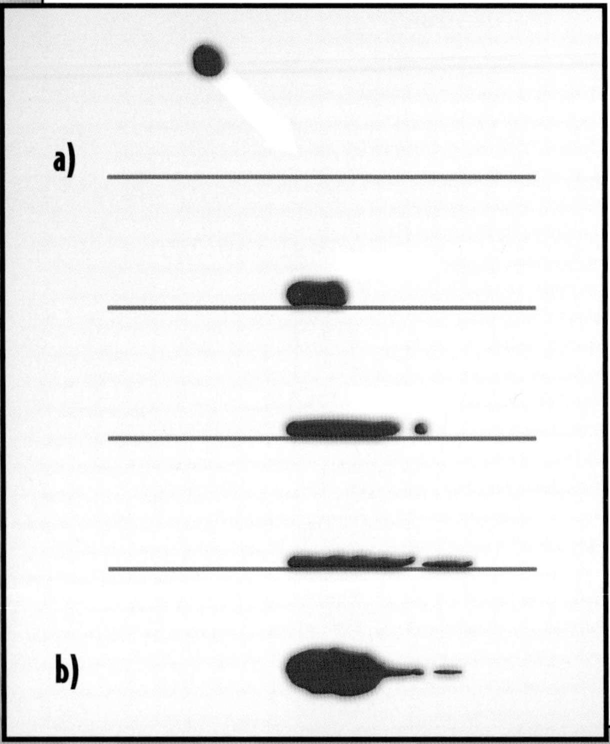

a)

b)

Figure 2.
a) This side view shows a blood drop moving toward a surface at an angle. The blood drop hits the surface and a tail forms. The tail points in the direction of travel.

b) This top view of the blood drop shows the starting drop and the tail.

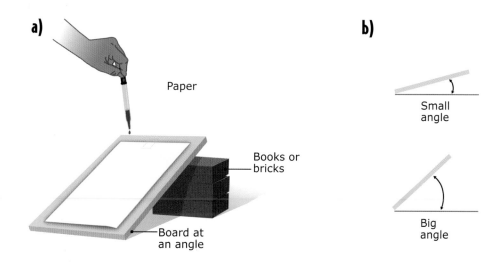

a)

Paper

Books or bricks

Board at an angle

b)

Small angle

Big angle

Figure 3. How does angle affect the spatter pattern?

Ideas for Science Fair Projects

- Compare spatter patterns of drops falling from different heights onto different surfaces. You might try wood, concrete, asphalt, plastic, cardboard, or waxed floors. Are the patterns different than the ones you have seen?

- Compare spatter patterns of drops at different horizontal speeds falling onto different surfaces. Are the patterns different from the ones you have seen?

❀ 1-2 Blood Types and Crime

Not all human blood is the same. A person's blood is one of four different types—A, B, AB, or O. Blood contains cells. There are red blood cells and white blood cells. The cells are in a fluid called plasma.

A simple test can be used to find a person's blood type. Two drops of blood from the person are placed on a microscope slide (see Figure 4a). A drop of A plasma is added to one drop. A drop of B plasma is added to the other drop. Figure 4b shows what happens to red blood cells for each of the four blood types after the plasma has been added, as seen through a microscope.

The four blood types react differently to A plasma and B plasma. Type A red blood cells form clumps in B plasma but remain apart in A plasma. Type B red blood cells clump together in A plasma but not in B plasma. AB red blood cells clump in both plasmas, and type O blood cells do not clump in either plasma.

a)

Figure 4.
a) Two drops of blood were placed on a microscope slide.

b)

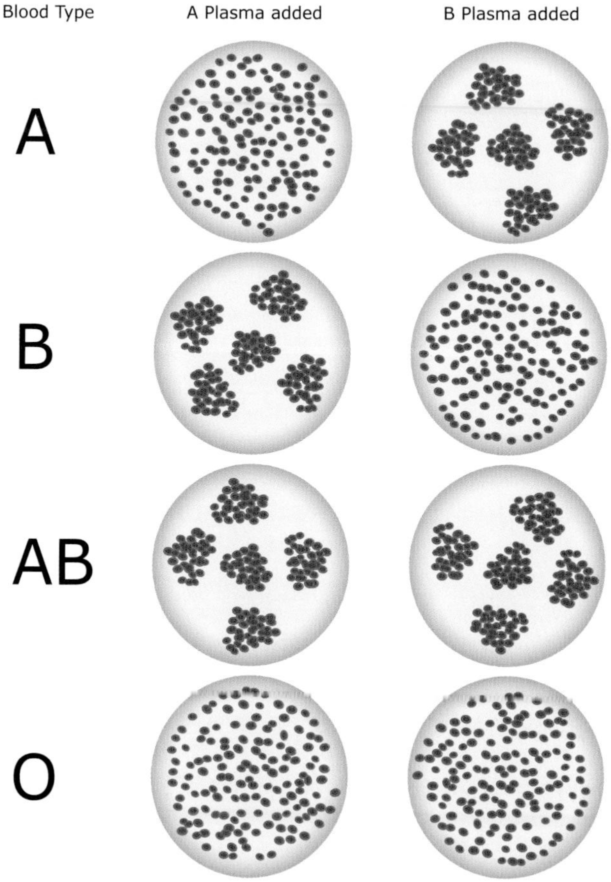

Blood Type	A Plasma added	B Plasma added
A		
B		
AB		
O		

b) Different blood types respond to A plasma and B plasma, as seen through a microscope.

Table 1. Blood type in the world population.

BLOOD TYPE	PERCENTAGE OF PEOPLE WITH THAT BLOOD TYPE
AB	3
B	9
A	42
O	46

Table 1 shows the percentage of people in the world who have each blood type. As you can see, type O blood is the most common, and type AB blood is the least common.

1 Blood is collected at a crime scene. It is taken to a crime lab and tested. The test shows that it is type AB.

2 A suspect is arrested. Two drops of his blood are placed on a microscope slide. A plasma is added to one drop. B plasma is added to the other drop. The result, seen through a microscope, is shown in Figure 5.

What is the suspect's blood type?

Does this test prove that the suspect is guilty? Does it prove that the suspect is innocent?

What would you suggest be done next?

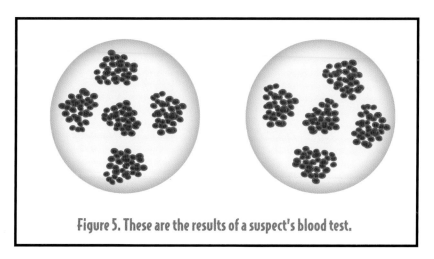

Figure 5. These are the results of a suspect's blood test.

Idea for a Science Fair Project

There are genes for types A, B, and O. Design and make demonstrations to show how blood types are inherited.

A Crime to Solve:
Spattered Blood From a Crime Scene

As a forensic expert on blood evidence, you have been asked to examine the bloodstain shown in the photograph below. The criminal, who was wounded by the victim's scratches, ran from the scene. The police want to know in which direction he ran, to the right or to the left. What do you tell them?

In which direction did the criminal run?

Using Bodies to Solve Crimes

If a dead body is found at a crime scene, it will be examined by a medical examiner. This doctor examines the dead body. He or she will try to figure out the time and cause of death. Weapons leave wounds. The wounds often make the cause of death obvious. Deaths due to poisoning, smothering, smoke inhalation, and other internal injuries are harder to figure out. In those cases, the victim's blood, lungs, and heart may need to be examined.

Estimating time of death may be difficult. Rigor mortis (stiffening of the muscles) begins about three hours after death. If there is no rigor mortis, the death probably occurred within the previous three hours. Rigor mortis starts in the face and slowly spreads to the arms. After twelve hours, the entire body will be rigid. Rigor mortis usually begins to disappear after two to three days. If the entire body is rigid, the time of death was probably twelve to seventy-two hours before the examination.

Gravity affects a dead person's blood. The blood slowly settles to the lowest parts of the body. If the body is on its back, blood settles in the small of the back and on the back of the neck and thighs. The blood of a facedown body settles to the front of the body. The settled blood gives the skin a bruised (bluish) appearance.

Following death, the body's temperature usually begins to fall. Normal body temperature is about 98.6°F (37°C). (Some people normally have higher or lower body temperature.) The temperature of a dead body drops about 1.5 degrees every hour. Medical examiners estimate time of death using the following rule:

Number of hours since death = (98.6°F minus dead body's temperature) divided by 3/2 (or 1.5°/hr)

Suppose the dead body's temperature is 95.6°F. The estimated time of death would be:

$$(98.6 - 95.6) = 3.0$$

$$3.0 \div 3/2 = 2 \text{ hours}$$

As you will find, many factors can affect this rule.

2-1 Time of Death and Body Temperature

How fast the temperature of a dead body drops depends on surrounding conditions. It does not always drop 1.5 degrees per hour for the first few hours. To see why, you can do experiments.

1 Record the temperature of the air in the room where you will be experimenting.

2 Add one cup of hot tap water to a plastic container. Place the thermometer in the water.

3 When the water is about 100°F, begin recording its temperature every five minutes. Continue to do this for an hour.

4 Plot a graph of the water's temperature versus time. A sample graph is shown in

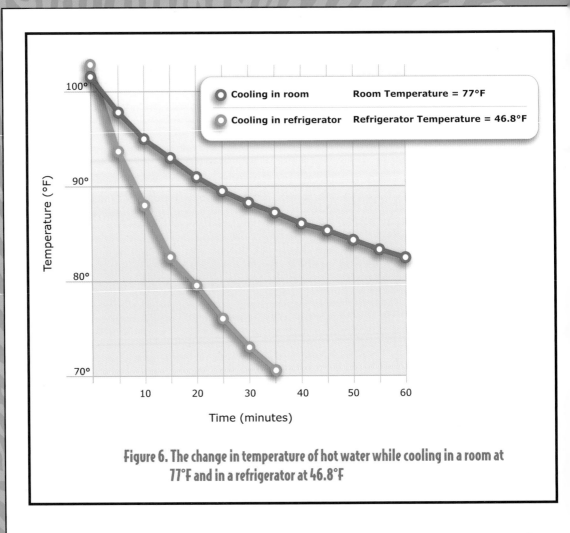

Figure 6. The change in temperature of hot water while cooling in a room at 77°F and in a refrigerator at 46.8°F

Figure 6. Compare your graph with this one. Is your graph similar?

Could the temperature of the air around a body affect its cooling rate?

5 To find out, record the temperature inside a refrigerator. Repeat this experiment, but this time put the water and thermometer in the refrigerator.

A sample graph is the lower curve in Figure 6. Compare your graph with this. Are the graphs similar?

Suppose a dead body was found in snow. Do you think it would have cooled faster than 1.5 degrees per hour?

Suppose a dead body was found in the desert where the temperature was 100°F or more. How might the body's temperature change over time?

Ideas for Science Fair Projects

- Could the amount of surface (surface area) exposed to the air affect cooling rates? Design and do an experiment to find out.

- Fat and clothing are insulators. They reduce the flow of heat. How might fat or clothing affect a body's change in temperature? Design and do experiments to find out. Foam coffee cups, newspaper, or cloth can provide insulation.

A Crime to Solve: A Body Is Found

You are the local medical examiner. A body is found beside an old country road. You are called to examine the body.

It is the evening of a hot summer day. The air temperature is still 95°F. The body is facedown. There appear to be bruises—bluish skin—on the small of the back and on the back of the neck and thighs. You find the temperature of the dead body to be 95.6°F. Except for the feet, the body is in a state of rigor mortis. You believe the time of death is about twelve hours ago. You write a note, "Someone touched the body before I arrived."

You question all those present. No one at the scene claims to have touched the body.

Your assistant estimates the time of death to be two hours ago. She shows you the following calculations:

$$98.6° - 95.6° = 3°$$
$$3° \div 1.5°/hr = 2 \text{ hours}$$

In your report, you record time of death to be about twelve hours before the examination. You also request that a forensic scientist look for fingerprints and trace evidence (hairs, fibers, skin cells, etc.) on the body. Why did you not accept your assistant's estimate? Why did you request a search for fingerprints and other evidence on the body?

Not an Accident

In 1925, Petrus Hauptfleisch, a native of South Africa, killed a woman. Her body lay facedown for several hours before Petrus returned to stage an accident. To make the accident believable, he placed her on her back.

The medical examiner saw that blood had collected in the front of her body. He realized that the body had been turned. The attempt to make the death appear accidental was discovered. Petrus was found guilty of murder.

3

Using Bones to Solve Crimes

Some scientists study fossilized bones of our ancient ancestors. They are called physical anthropologists. The FBI and other police departments often work with these scientists. When bones are found, there are many questions. Are the bones human? How old are they? Are they from a crime victim? If so, was the victim male or female? What was the person's race? Was he tall or short? Was he muscular? Physical anthropologists can answer such questions and more.

The bones of the pelvis are useful in determining whether the skeletal remains are those of a man or a woman. A woman's pelvis is wider and shallower than a man's (see Figure 7).

If a skeleton has teeth, dental records may help identify the remains. Height is easy to determine from a complete skeleton, but anthropologists use math to estimate height from partial skeletons. You can see how by doing an experiment.

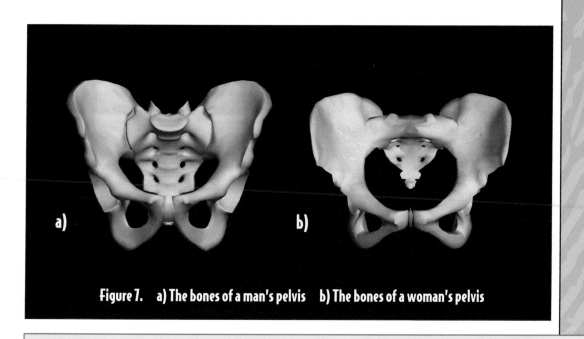

Figure 7.   a) The bones of a man's pelvis   b) The bones of a woman's pelvis

Sherlock Bones

In the 1930s, the FBI realized that anthropologists at the Smithsonian Institution in Washington, D.C., might help them solve crimes. In 1942, they hired T. Dale Stewart as a consultant. Stewart was the director of physical anthropology at the Smithsonian. Thirty years later, Smithsonian anthropologist Larry Angel was involved in many cases. He helped answer the FBI's numerous questions about skeletal remains. He was so involved, crime reporters called him "Sherlock Bones."

3-1 Finding Height by Measuring Bones

Anthropologists can estimate the height of a crime victim from skeletal remains (bones). Suppose a human femur (upper leg bone), the longest bone in the body, is found (see Figure 8). An anthropologist can estimate the victim's height using the following formula:

victim's height = length of femur (in inches) × 2.38 + 24.2 inches

If the femur is 18 inches long, the estimated height of the victim would be 67 inches (5 feet, 7 inches):

estimated height = (18 in × 2.38) + 24.2 in = 42.8 in

42.8 in + 24.2 in = 67.0 in

You may be able to make estimates of height by measuring other bones.

1 Have someone measure your ulna (see Figure 8). It is the bone that goes from your elbow to the small bump on the outside

of your wrist. How long is your ulna?

2 Divide your height in inches by the length of your ulna. Suppose your height is 54 inches and your ulna is 9 inches long. Then 54 inches ÷ 9 inches = 6. The number you find may be different.

3 You can use the number you found to estimate the height of other people. Just measure their ulnas. Suppose the number you found was 6 and someone's ulna is 8 inches long. You would estimate their height to be 6 × 8 inches, or 48 inches.

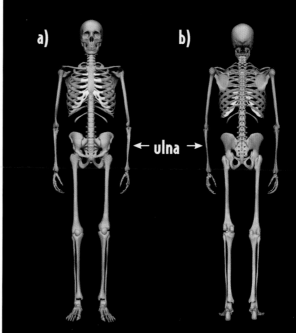

Figure8. The human skeleton: a) front view b) rear view

4 Use this method to estimate the height of a number of people. Then measure their heights. How accurate are your estimates?

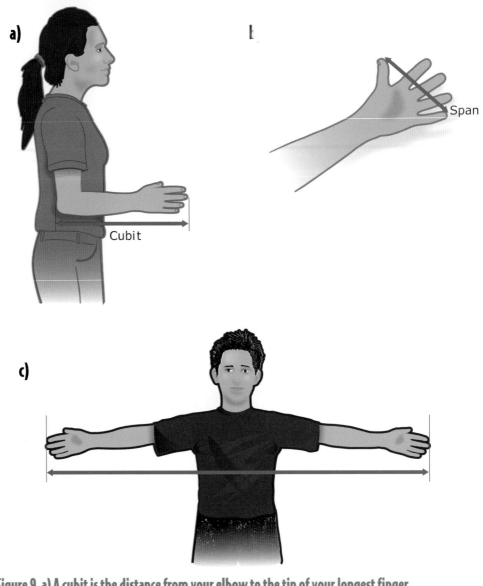

a)

Cubit

b)

Span

c)

Figure 9. a) A cubit is the distance from your elbow to the tip of your longest finger.
b) Your span is the distance across your outstretched hand. How does it compare
with the cubit?
c) How does the distance across your outstretched arms compare with your height?

5 Try other ways of estimating a person's height. What numbers do you get when you divide your height by your cubit? By your span? By the distance across your outstretched arms? (See Figure 9.) Use those numbers to estimate the heights of other people.

Ideas for Science Fair Projects

- Do the methods you used to estimate height work better for adults than for children? Do experiments to find out.

- Can you estimate a person's height by the length of their feet?

- Can you make a good estimate of a barefoot person's height by measuring the distance from his knee to the floor?

3-2 Be a Chicken-Bone Anthropologist

1 Next time chicken is served at your home, ask your parent to save one of the bones. Explain that you are going to be a chicken-bone anthropologist. You will try to identify the bone.

2 After your parent gives you the bone, examine it carefully. Try to identify the bone using the chicken skeleton shown in Figure 10. What bone do you think it is? What makes you think so?

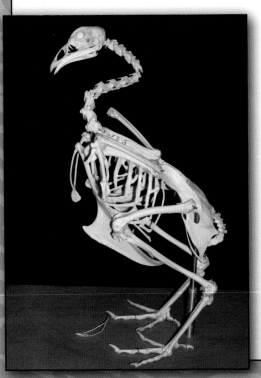

Figure 10.
A chicken skeleton

A Crime to Solve: Missing Person

A man's wife has disappeared. He told friends that she had gone to Europe to visit family and former basketball teammates. (She was a college basketball player who was about six feet, two inches tall.) Two years later, she has still not returned. Neighbors are suspicious and ask police to investigate.

THINGS YOU WILL NEED:
- Figure 7 (page 27)
- Figure 11

Police search the house and property. In the woods behind the man's house, they find a section of ground that appears different from its surroundings. They dig up the ground and find a skeleton.

As a forensic anthropologist, you are asked to examine the skeleton. You carefully examine the bones shown in Figure 11. You measure the femur and find its length to be 21 inches. What do you tell police?

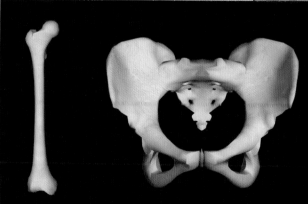

Figure 11. Using these bones, can you determine height, gender, and cause of death?

4

Using Bullets to Solve Crimes

Ballistics is the study of bullets and guns. Forensic experts in ballistics have solved many crimes. They often use a particular piece of evidence: the markings on bullets that have been fired from a gun.

When rifles and pistols are made, the barrels (Figure 12) are drilled out with a cutting tool. The tool makes a spiral groove like the threads on a screw, only farther apart. The tool also leaves ridges and grooves inside the barrel. When a bullet is fired, the spiral groove makes the bullet spin as it leaves the barrel. A spinning bullet travels faster and straighter than one that doesn't spin. Bullets are made slightly wider than the gun's barrel. As a result, the bullet rubs against the ridges and grooves as it leaves the weapon.

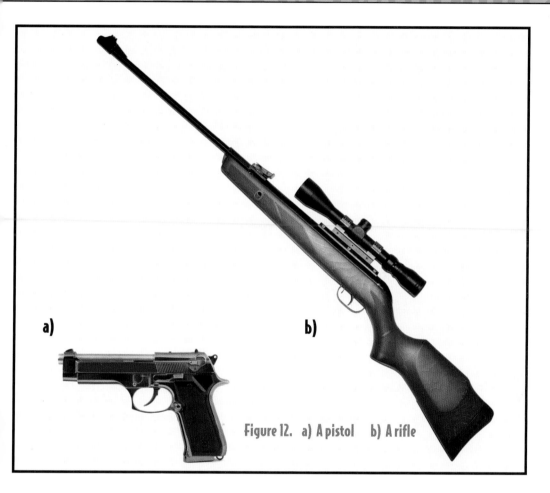

a)

b)

Figure 12. a) A pistol   b) A rifle

The rubbing against the ridges in the barrel produces striations—stripes—on the bullet. These striations are like the gun's fingerprints. No two guns produce the same bullet markings. Why? Because as the cutting tool wears with each drilling, it leaves slightly different ridges and grooves.

4-1 Why Bullets Are Made to Spin

THINGS YOU WILL NEED:

- football
- a person who can throw a spiral pass with a football (optional)

A bullet is spinning when it comes out of a gun barrel. The spiral groove in the barrel makes the bullet turn as it is fired. By the time it leaves the barrel, it is spinning very fast.

To see why guns are made to make bullets spin, you need only a football.

1 You may have seen a quarterback at a football game throw a spiral pass. If you can throw a spiral pass, you are ready to start. If not, ask someone who can throw a spiral pass to help you.

2 Use a football to throw a spiral pass (see Figure 13a). Notice how the ball travels smoothly and swiftly through the air. A bullet from a gun moves in a similar way, only faster. A spiraling football and a bullet both spin rapidly as they move through air. We say they have angular (spin) momentum.

This momentum keeps an object moving steadily along a straight path.

3 Now throw the ball so that it doesn't spin. Put your hand on the side of the ball (see Figure 13b) and throw it like a basketball. A bullet would travel in a similar way if it didn't spiral. The muskets used in the American Revolution did not have spiraled barrels. As a result, they were not very accurate from more than a few feet.

4 How far can you or your helper throw a spiral pass? How far will the ball travel if you throw it like a basketball?

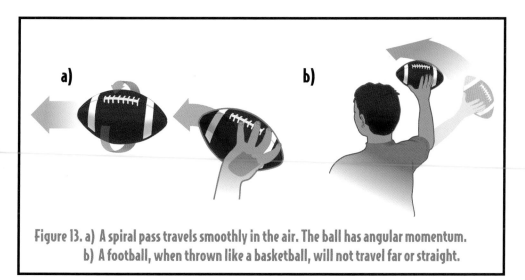

Figure 13. a) A spiral pass travels smoothly in the air. The ball has angular momentum.
b) A football, when thrown like a basketball, will not travel far or straight.

4-2 Bullet Holes and Angles

Forensic scientists can learn a lot by looking at the holes made by bullets. They can often tell whether a bullet hit a body or material at an angle or straight-on (at 90 degrees). They can sometimes map the path that a bullet traveled. You can see how they get such information by doing experiments.

1   Find a large nail 3½ or more inches long. Push the nail straight through a piece of thin cardboard at a 90-degree angle (see Figure 14a). Then push the same nail through the same cardboard at a sharp angle (Figure 14b).

2   Look at the two holes. How do they differ? How could police decide whether a bullet entered something straight-on or at an angle?

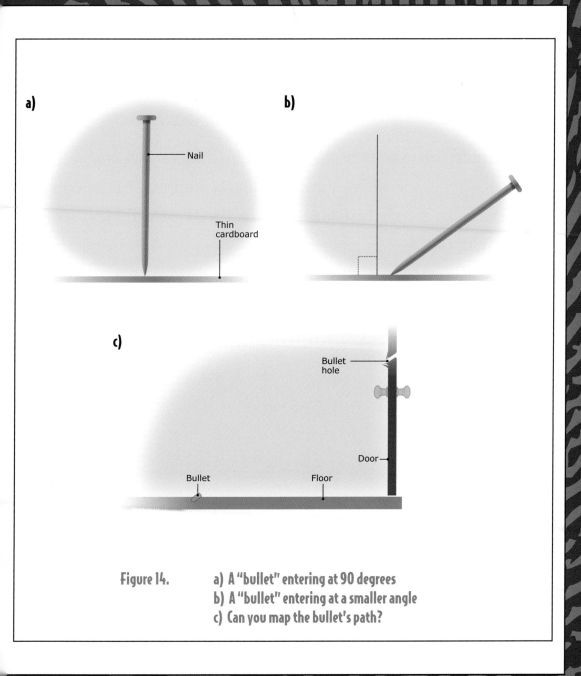

Figure 14.   a) A "bullet" entering at 90 degrees
b) A "bullet" entering at a smaller angle
c) Can you map the bullet's path?

By finding a bullet hole and the remains of the bullet, police can usually map the bullet's path. Using that information, they can tell from which direction the gun was fired.

3 Figure 14c shows a door through which a bullet was fired and the floor where the bullet finally stopped. Use a copier to make a copy of Figure 14c. DO NOT MAKE MARKS IN THIS BOOK!

4 Use a pencil and a ruler to draw the bullet's path from the door to the floor.

5 Using a protractor, find the angle at which the bullet entered the floor.

Ideas for a Science Fair Project

- The range of a water pistol is the distance the water "bullets" travel before hitting the ground or floor. How is the range of a water pistol affected by the angle at which it is fired?

- Do any two or more firing angles have the same range? If so, explain why.

A Crime to Solve: Did the Bullets Come From the Suspect's Gun?

A gun was fired at a store clerk during a robbery. The bullet was found at the crime scene. A suspect has been arrested. A gun and bullets found in his possession are being held as evidence.

As a ballistics expert, you have been asked, "Did the bullet fired at the robbery come from the suspect's gun?"

You fire a bullet from the suspect's gun into a deep tank of water. The water stops the bullet, which you remove from the water.

You place the two bullets under a comparison microscope. This allows you to compare the striations on the two bullets. What you see is shown in the photograph. What do you conclude?

Do the striations in these two bullets match?

Guilty

In 1920, Nicola Sacco and Bartolomeo Vanzetti were arrested. They were charged with the murder of two men shot during a robbery in South Braintree, Massachusetts. Both men owned guns. A bullet found in one of the victims was the same caliber (size) as one found in Sacco's pocket. This evidence led to their conviction.

Because the men were immigrants, many believed they had come to the United States to overthrow the government. Others felt they had not had a fair trial. In 1927, the governor of Massachusetts appointed a committee to investigate. The committee asked Calvin Goddard, a firearms expert, to examine the evidence. Goddard fired a bullet from Sacco's gun into a tank of cotton. He then examined that bullet and the one found in the victim using a comparison microscope. Both Goddard and Augustus Gill, another firearms expert who had been hired by Sacco and Vanzetti's lawyers, agreed. The striations on the two bullets matched. Both had been fired by Sacco's gun. The conviction stood. Both Sacco and Vanzetti were confirmed guilty.

Answers

1-2: Figure 5 shows that the suspect's blood reacted with the A Plasma and the B Plasma, so his blood type is AB. However, it does not *prove* that he is guilty, since 3 percent of the world's population has type AB blood. Police should investigate further.

1-3: The tail of the bloodstain is to the left, so you conclude that the criminal was running in that direction (left).

2-2: Because it is such a hot day, the body would not cool as quickly as normal. Your assistant's formula does not apply under such conditions. Since rigor mortis is almost complete, you estimate time of death to be about twelve hours ago.

Because blood settled to the back of the body, it must have been on its back. Someone turned the body. That person may have left fingerprints, hair, or other trace evidence on the body.

3-3: The bone you measured was a femur, the longest bone in the human body. To find the height of the person whose skeleton was found, you use the formula:

victim's height = (length of femur in inches × 2.38) + 24.2 inches

You find that

(21 inches × 2.38) + 24.2 inches = 74.2 inches

Since 74.2 inches is about six feet, two inches, the skeleton matches the height of the missing woman. You also see that the pelvic bone is that of a female. You tell police that the skeleton could be the remains of the missing person.

4-3: The striations match, so you conclude that both bullets were fired from the suspect's gun.

Words to Know

ballistics—The study of bullets and guns, which are often involved in crimes.

blood type—One of the four types of human blood: A, B, AB, or O.

comparison microscope—An instrument that combines the enlarged images of two microscopes. When their images are combined, two objects, such as two bullets, can be compared by viewing them side by side.

crime scene—The place where a crime happened.

DNA—The spiral-shaped chemical (deoxyribonucleic acid) found in the nucleus of most living cells. Except for identical twins, no two people have the same DNA.

evidence—Things that can be used to solve crimes and to convict criminals in a court of law, such as fingerprints, hair, and blood.

forensic science—The science used to investigate and solve crimes. It is also used in courts of law.

forensic scientist—A person who uses science to solve crimes and whose findings may be used as evidence in court.

Words to Know (Continued)

luminol—A chemical that reacts with red blood cells. The reaction makes a bluish glow that can be seen in the dark. It can reveal even small traces of blood that cannot normally be seen.

medical examiner—A doctor who investigates deaths and tries to establish their time and cause.

physical anthropologist—A scientist who searches for and studies the fossilized bones of our human ancestors. Physical anthropologists often help police identify and study skeletal remains (bones) discovered at what may be crime scenes.

rigor mortis—A stiffening of the muscles that takes place after a person dies.

striations (on bullets)—Striped markings left on bullets as they travel through a gun barrel.

Further Reading

Books

Bardhan-Quallen, Sudipta. *Championship Science Fair Projects: 100 Sure-to-Win Experiments.* New York: Sterling, 2004.

Denega, Danielle. *Gut-eating Bugs: Maggots Reveal the Time of Death.* New York: Franklin Watts, 2007.

Fridell, Ron. *Forensic Science.* Minneapolis: Lerner Publications Company, 2007.

Hopping, Lorraine Jean. *Crime Scene Science: Investigating a Crime Scene.* Milwaukee: World Almanac Library, 2007.

Rhadigan, Joe, and Rain Newcomb. *Prize-Winning Science Fair Projects for Curious Kids.* New York: Lark Books, 2004.

Internet Addresses

Access Excellence: The Mystery Spot
http://www.accessexcellence.org/AE/mspot/

FBI Youth
http://www.fbi.gov/ds/6th12th/6th12th.htm

Who Dunnit?
http://www.cyberbee.com/whodunnit/crime.html

Index